In the Spotlight

Anthony Rizzo

by Kaitlyn Duling

Bullfrog Books

Ideas for Parents and Teachers

Bullfrog Books let children practice reading informational text at the earliest reading levels. Repetition, familiar words, and photo labels support early readers.

Before Reading

- Discuss the cover photo. What does it tell them?

- Look at the picture glossary together. Read and discuss the words.

Read the Book

- "Walk" through the book and look at the photos. Let the child ask questions. Point out the photo labels.

- Read the book to the child, or have him or her read independently.

After Reading

- Prompt the child to think more. Ask: What did you know about Anthony Rizzo before reading this book? What more would you like to learn about him after reading it?

j biog
R520d
Rizzo

Bullfrog Books are published by Jump!
5357 Penn Avenue South
Minneapolis, MN 55419
www.jumplibrary.com

Library of Congress Cataloging-in-Publication Data

Names: Duling, Kaitlyn, author.
Title: Anthony Rizzo / by Kaitlyn Duling.
Description: Bullfrog Books edition.
Minneapolis, Minnesota: Bullfrog Books
are published by Jump!, [2019]
Series: In the spotlight | Audience: Ages: 5–8.
Audience: Grades: K to Grade 3. | Includes index.
Identifiers: LCCN 2018018926 (print)
LCCN 2018022415 (ebook)
ISBN 9781641282062 (ebook)
ISBN 9781641282048 (hardcover: alk. paper)
ISBN 9781641282055 (paperback)
Subjects: LCSH: Rizzo, Anthony, 1989
Juvenile literature. | Baseball players
United States—Biography—Juvenile literature.
Classification: LCC GV865.R498 (ebook)
LCC GV865.R498 D85 2018 (print) | DDC 796.357092 [B]—dc23
LC record available at https://lccn.loc.gov/2018018926

Editor: Susanne Bushman
Designer: Molly Ballanger

Photo Credits: Jamie Squire/Getty, cover, 4, 23tl; Rich Pilling/Getty, 1; Daniel Bartel/Getty, 3; Ron Vesely/Getty, 5, 12–13, 23tr; Jamie Sabau/Getty, 6–7, 23bl; Steve Broer/Shutterstock, 7; Kirk Irwin/Getty, 8; Ronald C. Modra/Getty, 9; LG Patterson/Getty, 10–11, 23br; Alex Trautwig/Getty, 11, 18, 19, 22t, 22br; David Banks/Getty, 14–15; Melanie Stetson Freeman/Getty, 16–17; Jon Durr/Getty, 20–21; Andy Hayt/Getty, 22bl; Dylan Buell/Getty, 24.

Printed in the United States of America at Corporate Graphics in North Mankato, Minnesota.

Table of Contents

Look! It is Anthony Rizzo!

He is famous.

Why?

He plays for the MLB.

What position does he play?

First base.

He catches.

first base

bat

He bats, too.

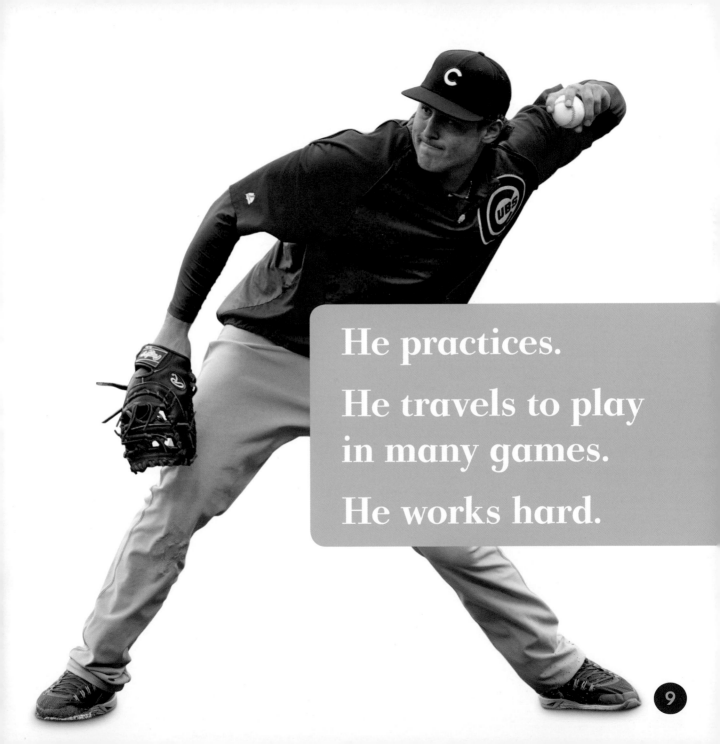

He practices.

He travels to play in many games.

He works hard.

Anthony ·······▶

His team won the
World Series.

When? In 2016.

Wow! Go Cubs!

He helps raise money.

He wants to help cure cancer.

Why? He had cancer, too.

Stand Up 2 Cancer

I STAND UP FOR My Family
S↑2C standup2cancer.org

I STAND UP FOR DELIA DAVIS
S↑2C standup2cancer.org

13

He lets kids
on the field.

Why?

He signs balls
for them.

Fans love Anthony.

fans

He even won an award.

award

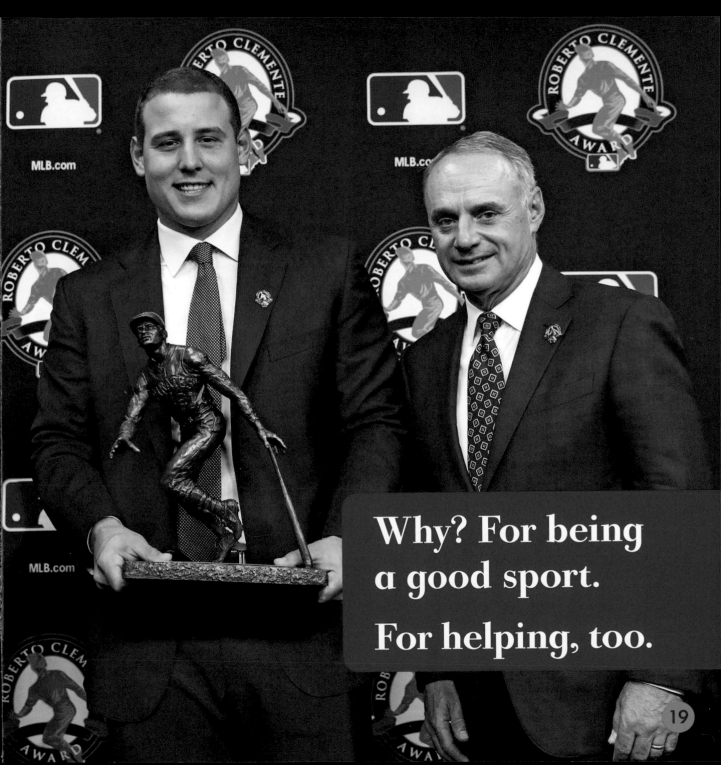

Why? For being a good sport. For helping, too.

Anthony is a great player.
He is a great person, too.

Key Events

August 8, 1989:
Anthony Vincent Rizzo is born in Fort Lauderdale, Florida.

January 6, 2012:
The San Diego Padres trade Anthony to the Chicago Cubs.

October 27, 2017:
Anthony wins the Roberto Clemente Award for being a good sport and being involved in his community.

November 2, 2016:
Anthony and the Chicago Cubs win the World Series for the first time in 108 years. Anthony makes a catch at first base for the final out of the series.

December 6, 2010:
Anthony joins the San Diego Padres.

May 8, 2017:
The Anthony Rizzo Family Foundation announces a $3.5 million donation to Lurie Children's Hospital in Chicago, Illinois.

Picture Glossary

famous
Very well-known to many people.

MLB
Major League Baseball;
the professional baseball
organization in North America.

position
A particular role on a team.

World Series
A series of championship games
played by professional baseball
teams every year.

Index

To Learn More

FACT SURFER

Finding more information is as easy as 1, 2, 3.

❶ Go to www.factsurfer.com

❷ Enter "AnthonyRizzo" into the search box.

❸ Click the "Surf" button to see a list of websites.